I AM THE NORMAL ONE

The funniest Jurgen Klopp quotes... ever!

by Gordon Law

About the author

Gordon Law is a freelance journalist and editor who has previously covered football for the *South London Press*, the *Premier League*, *Virgin Media* and a number of English national newspapers and magazines. He has also written several books on the beautiful game.

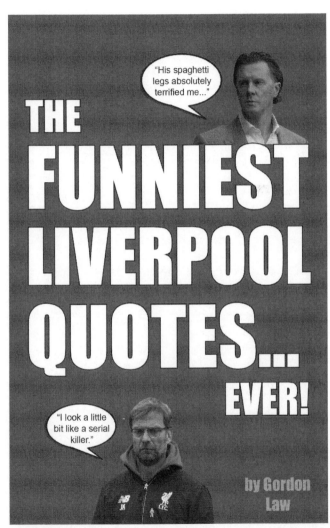

Also available to buy

Printed in the United States of America
ISBN-13: 978-1539644408
ISBN-10: 1539644405

Photos courtesy of: Michael Hulf.

Proofreaders: Hywel Jones, Stewart Coggin.

Contents

Introduction

Jurgen Klopp announced himself as 'the Normal One' after being unveiled as the new manager of Liverpool.

Not since Jose Mourinho's arrival at Chelsea – where he referred to himself as 'the Special One' – has a footballing personality captured the public's imagination.

Though Klopp played down that comparison in his own inimitable style, there can be no doubt his fantastic achievements with Borussia Dortmund make him one of the game's finest managers.

He led Dortmund to back-to-back Bundesliga titles, domestic cup wins and transformed them into a major force in Europe, while playing an attacking, exciting brand of football.

Klopp, like Mourinho, is not only a brilliant coach and master tactician but a charismatic, eccentric and entertaining figure.

With his trademark beard, baseball cap and infectious, toothy grin, Klopp has amused us all with an endless supply of hilarious quotes from his time with Dortmund and now Liverpool.

Whether it's discussing his shaving habits, threatening to "eat a broomstick", describing a new signing as fitting in his team "like an arse on a bucket" or blasting reporters, Klopp is box-office gold.

Many of the German's weird and wonderful observations can be found here in this unique collection of quips and quotes. Enjoy!

Gordon Law

Klopp on... Borussia Dortmund

"None of my teams has ever played 'lawn chess'."

Speaking to the media during his unveiling as the new manager of Dortmund

"I place 0.0 per cent faith in his statistics and he knows it too. I've said it to his face so I feel perfectly comfortable saying it in public."

Klopp doesn't agree with sports scientist and football stats expert Dr Roland Loy who has worked for German TV

"You get a better view, but otherwise it's crap."

The manager on being forced to watch games from the stand

Klopp on... Borussia Dortmund

"I compare it to a bobsled race. We had a great start – should we then get out while racing and explain how well we started?"

The German responding to reporters' questions on how well Borussia Dortmund have begun the season

"When Dortmund last won here 19 years ago, most of my players were still being breast-fed."

Klopp is elated to have finally defeated Bayern Munich in 2011

"Mkhitaryan fits us like an arse on a bucket. What he offers is exactly what we need."

The manager's wonderful description of the £24million acquisition Henrikh Mkhitaryan. This phrase is actually a fairly common working-class German colloquialism with the English equivalent being 'fits like a glove'

"Better a table leader for one night than never."

Dortmund move top of the league after eight games for the first time in the season with a victory over FC Cologne

"[Mario] Gotze has gone because he is [Pep] Guardiola's personal chosen signing and he wants to play with Guardiola, in his style. I can't make myself 15cm shorter or start speaking Spanish. I cannot preach a football based on quick transitions and then [suddenly] start playing tiki-taka."

Klopp laments the loss of Mario Gotze to rivals Bayern

"If that's not a bullsh*t story, I'll eat a broomstick!"

On Mats Hummels being linked with a transfer to Manchester United

"If, in the last four years, Barcelona were the first team I saw playing when I was four years of age – this serenity of football, they win 5-0, 6-0 – I would have played tennis."

On the challenge of overcoming the might of Barcelona

"Kevin, you are one of the only ones who looks better with a mask than without one."

On Kevin Grosskreutz wearing a protective mask due to a nose injury

"At the moment, they are like the Chinese in the business world. They look at what others are doing and copy it, just with more money."
On Bayern Munich's philosophy

"I got more in life than I was ever supposed to get – family, money, football. None of my teachers, or my parents, ever believed this would happen to me. So how can this perfect life of mine be spoilt because they take our players?"
Klopp on the big guns swooping for Dortmund's stars

"If all these players had stayed, I would have to go because there'd be nothing new. If I say, 'Go left!' They would say, 'You've told us that 200 times. We don't want to hear your voice any more'. That's life."

Klopp is realistic about his best players leaving Dortmund

"If this was our problem, I'd be the first to give the players a kick up the backside each day of the week."

He is asked if the Dortmund players could get by on giving only 95 per cent

Klopp on... Borussia Dortmund

"Well, if we are honest, if Bayern wins, I would really like it. But it's not that I'm sitting in front of the TV on Saturday evening and wearing Bayern things... But now you're facing Casablanca. If Humphrey Bogart doesn't play – that's the last time I heard about Casablanca."

Klopp plays down the credibility of the FIFA Club World Cup as Bayern play Moroccan side Raja Casablanca

I AM THE NORMAL ONE

"We're facing the greatest challenge there is in football: to play against an Italian team that only needs a draw."

Klopp on the daunting prospect of playing against Juventus in the last 16 of the Champions League

"UEFA-Cup feeling? Is that like heartburn?"

When the manager is asked by a journalist about his first foray into Europe with Dortmund

Klopp on... Borussia Dortmund

"I told them that I want some messages and always a little check-up – 'I'm fine, it's OK' – after the games especially."

Klopp requests a reassuring text from his players before returning from international duty

"The best news today is that football is over for 2014 and any criticism that we receive now is justified. We are standing here like complete idiots and it's completely our own fault."

He is only too aware of Dortmund's shortcomings in the 2014 calendar year

"Shinji Kagawa is one of the best players in the world and he now plays 20 minutes at Manchester United – on the left wing. My heart breaks. Really, I have tears in my eyes. Central midfield is Shinji's best role. He's an offensive midfielder with one of the best noses for goal I ever saw."

Klopp feels Japanese midfielder Shinji Kagawa is being misused by Manchester United after his transfer in 2012

"It's as if someone has to play the world chess championship after 72 hours of sleep deprivation."

Describing Dortmund's fixture congestion

"I show my team very often Barcelona – but not the way they play. Just the way they celebrate goals. Goal no 5768 in the last few weeks and they go 'Yeeeess' like they never scored a goal. This is what I love about football. That's what you have to feel all the time. Until you die. And then everything is OK."

Barcelona's sustained hunger has Klopp looking on in admiration

"It could have been a bit warmer."

When asked by a reporter if beating Bayern 5-2 in the German Cup final could have been any better

"My English is not good enough to express this... I was really excited. I came in and saw the dressing room for the away team, and asked myself if I needed some colour to paint or something like this! The derby starts at this moment! You go into the dressing room, and you think, 'OK, they want to kick us!' It was historical."

Boss Klopp recounts his delight at visiting Anfield when his Dortmund side played Liverpool for a pre-season game

"Whoever says that this team has motivational problems suffers from Alzheimer's disease."

Klopp responds to a reporter who asked about Dortmund's inconsistency

Klopp on... Borussia Dortmund

"I'm not looking for a fight, so I will even answer the stupid questions. If you say we've been 'found out', what does that say about opposition coaches for the last few years? Were they unable to see what our game is?"

Klopp angrily hitting back at suggestions that Dortmund had been 'found out'

"Every time one of these guys extends here, it's like a second birthday for me."

He is chuffed whenever one of his Dortmund stars snubs another club to sign a new deal

"We took the team to a lake in Sweden where there was no electricity. We went for five days without food. They had to do this [he casts off an imaginary fishing rod]. The other coaches said, 'Don't you think it's better to train playing football?' No. I wanted the team to feel that they can survive everything. My assistant coach thinks I'm an idiot. He asks if we can train there. No. Can we run there? No. But we can swim and fish! But it was brilliant. We were like Bravehearts. You can stick a knife in me here – no problem. We went to the Bundesliga and people could not believe how strong we were."

Klopp recalls the time he took his Mainz squad on an unusual pre-season trip in 2004

Klopp on... Borussia Dortmund

"I told my players during the break: Since we're here anyway, we might actually play a bit of football."

Klopp used a sarcastic half-time team talk to motivate his players

"I'd have to sell my whole team!"

A reporter asks if Klopp was going to sign Zlatan Ibrahimovic for Dortmund

"We will wait for him like a good wife waiting for her husband who is in jail."

On Mats Hummels after the defender's latest breakdown through injury

"It is not my sport. I don't like winning with 80 per cent [possession]. Sorry that is not enough for me. Fighting football, not serenity football, that is what I like. What we call in German 'English' – rainy day, heavy pitch, 5-5, everybody is dirty in the face and goes home and cannot play for weeks after."

On his rough-and-ready footballing philosophy

Klopp on... Borussia Dortmund

"Finishing the first half of the season in 17th place felt like how going on holiday and sleeping on a bed of nails must feel."

Klopp looks on as Dortmund plummet to second bottom at the halfway point of the 2014/15 campaign after finishing second the season before

"It's absolutely normal that people go different ways. At 18 I wanted to see the whole world. But I am only in Mainz and Dortmund since then and it's not the middle of the world. It's OK that they want to go to different places. But they get there and, sh*t, it's not the same."

The manager on players wanting to leave Dortmund for other clubs

"The fans should not only recognise us by our black and yellow jerseys. Even if we play in red, everyone in the stadium should think, 'Whoa, that can only be BVB'."

On creating a special brand of football at Dortmund

"I'm really surprised. I sent him a text message saying 'Why Schalke????????' with eight question marks, but I didn't hear back from him. He was a good lad, up until this morning."

Kevin-Prince Boateng is in the bad books after signing with big rivals Schalke

"Dujardin? Like the brandy? Congratulations! And you work as well..."

Klopp mistakes the surname of former Goal Germany editor Francois Duchateau for the name of a cognac manufacturer located near Dortmund

"If that's what Bayern wants... It's like James Bond – except they are the other guy [the villain]."

On Robert Lewandowski being chased by Bayern

"The same day you finally understand the game of football!"

When asked if striker Nelson Valdez would finally leave the club

"When we are there we don't want to be tourists."

Klopp wants Dortmund to seize their opportunity in the 2013 Champions League final at Wembley

"Who of the two teams can hurt the other most on the field."

When asked how Dortmund v Bayer Leverkusen will be decided

Klopp on... Borussia Dortmund

Now, I'm at the perfect club at the perfect time. In the future, if my English is better and someone asks me, maybe I'll come to the Premier League."

Flattered but spoken for – Klopp is happy at Dortmund but refuses to rule out England one day

Q: "If I were one of your players, what would you do now to get my adrenaline pumping?"

A: Klopp looked at the reporter for a second, then gave him a slap in the face

"Screw you. I like giving interviews to you as much as having toothache. Do you have to come here or what?"

A TV reporter catches Klopp in a bad mood when trying to ask him questions in a post-match interview

"I behaved like a monkey out there. I went too far."

Klopp reflects on being sent to the stands for angrily gesticulating at the fourth official when Neven Subotic was told he couldn't return to the pitch following a head injury

"We know about the reasons but we've also had injuries with the foot that we've never heard about. Sometimes one comes through the other."
Klopp, breaking out in laughter, describes the injury crisis at the club after a number of key players had spells out injured

"How do you explain to a blind person what colour is?"
Responding to a Schalke fan who wanted to know the secret of winning the title

"I didn't even watch the draw – I just knew we'd get Bayern. I instead watched Law & Order, which is on the peculiarities of the American legal system!"

Klopp is more interested in watching TV than following the German Cup semi-final draw

"We didn't practise with the heading pendulum. Unfortunately you can't set it that low."

On Japanese midfielder Shinji Kagawa scoring a header against FC Karpaty Lviv

"I didn't need glasses. If a player plants his right leg on the goal-line and clears the ball with his left, he'd have to belong to Cirque du Soleil for it not to be a goal."

A sarcastic Klopp on Bayern's Dante clearing Mats Hummel's header off the line in the 2014 German Cup final

"I have never in my life had to worry about title chances and calculating percentages was also not my area. We have to work, not calculate."

When asked about the likelihood of winning the league after a 2-0 success over Nuremberg halfway through the season

"We again made two serious mistakes and [then] got two goals back. This is the classic case: What we build with our hands, we knock down with our butts."

Klopp bemoans his Dortmund team's defending in a 2-2 draw against Stuttgart

"Today we had 20 people in front of our hotel… last time five. So, still not too many."

On Dortmund's return to London to play Arsenal a few months after their Wembley Champions League appearance

Klopp on... Borussia Dortmund

Interviewer: "This tie is over, isn't it?"

Klopp: "How could I justify picking up my pay cheque if I stand here and say the tie is over? It would be just as stupid as saying we're going to walk all over them [in the second leg]. I can always supply silly answers to silly questions. [Sarcastically] Yes, the tie is over, but we have to play them anyway."

Speaking after a 3-0 first-leg defeat to Real Madrid in 2014

"That was like Robin Hood taking from the rich."

Klopp is delighted with the 4-1 semi-final first-leg win over Real Madrid in the Champions League in 2013

"It makes me proud to hear that some Arsenal fans might want me, but it's not important for me to be proud. My mother is proud. It's a better feeling than if nobody knows me but it doesn't help me in the morning, it doesn't help me in the evening and it doesn't help me through the day."

The manager is philosophical about speculation linking him with a move to the Gunners

"More freak-show material."

Klopp fumes after conceding sloppy goals in the defeat to Eintracht Frankfurt

"People told me that if we'd won the DFB Cup this season, it would have been a bit of a cheesy ending. Perhaps a bit too American. I'm happy that we're all so realistic. It's better that way."

The manager reflects on the 3-1 German Cup final defeat to Wolfsburg

"Maybe that was the case when I was 17 or 18."

Klopp was asked if he was a 'one-night man' after Dortmund temporarily moved to the top of the table

"I made a deal with the players: if you can manage to run more than 118 kilometres in nine out of 10 games, you'll get an extra three days' holiday."

The manager's attempt at bribing his Dortmund players actually pays off

"Some might think, 'There's a real nice bloke, always in a good mood' and the others might say, 'That smug git has been getting on my bloody t*ts for years'."

Klopp knows he's a man who divides opinion

Klopp on... Borussia Dortmund

"We have a bow and arrow and if we aim well, we can hit the target. The problem is that Bayern has a bazooka. The probability that they will hit the target is clearly higher. But then Robin Hood was apparently quite successful."

Klopp describes how difficult it is to compete with the might of Bayern Munich each year in the Bundesliga

"If we end up second come the summer, then I'll fetch a bus and drive around my garden and party. If no one else can celebrate second place, I'll do it alone."

Finishing behind European giants Bayern is still seen as a fine achievement by Klopp

"Bayern want a decade of success like Barca. That's OK if you have the money because it increases the possibility of success. But it's not guaranteed. We are not a supermarket but they want our players because they know we cannot pay them the same money."

Klopp hits out at Bayern's big-spending transfer policy

"I know that my team cannot play the same cr*p twice in a row."

The boss after his side was defeated 3-0 by Nuremberg

Klopp on... Borussia Dortmund

"When I was a player there [at Mainz] we had 800 supporters on rainy Saturday afternoons and if we died, no one would notice or come to our funeral. But we loved the club and we have this same feeling at Dortmund. It's a very special club – a workers' club."

Klopp speaks about the bond he has forged with the Dortmund fans

Q: "Have you been taking Spanish lessons?"

A: "Yes – I can now say 'one beer please'."

Prior to his departure to Liverpool, Klopp is asked by a reporter if it is true he was looking to manage in La Liga

"The only thing I can say is that it was great. London is the town of the Olympic Games. The weather was good, everything is OK. Only the result is sh*t."

Klopp is magnanimous in defeat to Bayern in the 2013 Champions League final at Wembley

"Other mothers also have beautiful sons who can play a bit. To anyone who is feeling nervous I can only say, relax."

The manager tries to calm Dortmund fans after Mario Gotze decided he was leaving for Bayern

Klopp on... Borussia Dortmund

"How can anyone pay my salary if I say the tie is done. I would be just as stupid to say we are going to thrash them, but I'm not going to be able continue standing in this studio to be provoked into saying a stupid thing. For stupid questions I can give stupid answers. 'Mr Klopp, is it dumb?' I'm sorry, we're gonna have to show up!"

Klopp just before he walks out of a TV interview after being asked if Dortmund were "done" in the Champions League

"I don't want to have the most money because you get problems with this. If you have 25 super, super superstars each morning you get up hoping one of them is ill. Maybe today one of them, what's his name, will have a cold [he fakes a sneeze]. 'Ah, you, I'm sorry, you cannot play at the weekend'. You hope that because you need a reason to take him out of the team. I don't want these problems."

On managing a club with superstars

"There's no point pushing anyone into an office. I prefer no one talking than anyone spewing bullsh*t."

Klopp replies to critics who said there was no leadership on the pitch

Klopp on... Borussia Dortmund

"It was like a heart attack. It was one day after [Dortmund's Champions League quarter-final win over] Malaga. I had one day to celebrate and then somebody thought, 'Enough, go back down on the floor.' At our training ground [general manager] Michael Zorc walked in like somebody had died. He said, 'I have to tell you something. It's possible that…'"

Klopp speaks of his devastation when he heard Mario Gotze would be leaving

"You don't understand? What a pity? 'You should learn, there's a very good German explanation for some problems, 'Alles hat eine ende nur die wurst hat zwei'. 'Everything has an end except for a sausage has two'."

Klopp on the long-running Dortmund injury crisis

"I can see you have fun when you come to Dortmund. Maybe it's because of the beer!"

He says it's more than football that attracts people to Dortmund

"It's a little bit like when you are born and your mother is [He makes a face like a woman in child birth]. Then, you come out and you see the best of the world. It's very dark inside and we come out."

Klopp describes walking out of the narrow tunnel at Dortmund's Westfalenstadion stadium

"I don't know. If this is the case, then I think this club is worth falling in love with because this is pure football. It's not like a show or a big play like Romeo and Juliet or something like this."

When asked if the world is falling in love with Dortmund

"When I was younger, we always wanted to play in conditions like this, but we were not allowed to because mum didn't want to do all the washing. Now we can play in these conditions, but nobody wants to."

On his Dortmund side playing in the mud at SC Freiburg

"If it smells of sweat in here, it's me. The match was just so exciting!"

Klopp to Schalke manager Fred Rutten in the lift as they headed to the post-match press conference after a 3-3 draw

"It's why a main act had to leave. And that's me.

That's the devil of the good deed, so to speak."

Klopp on departing Dortmund

"Calm down, it's Christmas?"

Photo: Michael Hulf

Klopp on... Liverpool

I AM THE NORMAL ONE

"I am not going to call myself anything. I am a normal guy from the Black Forest. My mother is watching this press conference at home. If you are going to call me anything, call me the Normal One. I was a very average player and became a trainer in Germany with a special club."

The new Liverpool manager after being asked by reporters if he was also a 'special one'

"If one game should change my mind then I would be a real idiot."

When questioned by journalists if he was going to reconsider buying new players after losing to Burnley

"When you come for the first time in a new house, normally you have a present. I am not quite satisfied with my present tonight but it was only the first time and I will come again."

Klopp on his first home game in charge of Liverpool – a 1-1 draw against Rubin Kazan in the Europa League

"OK, it was not a masterclass, but come on, it was not boring either. It was not the worst day in my life. I would say 98 per cent OK, not perfect, the other two per cent, that is the problem of this game."

Klopp refuses to be downcast after the Rubin Kazan match

"A lot of people at UEFA watched it and said it was a normal challenge. That is no problem but they gave me three games just for my face in Naples."

Klopp says he is not surprised that Man United's Marouane Fellaini escaped punishment despite appearing to elbow Emre Can. He contrasted it with a ban he received for confronting the fourth official during a Dortmund loss to Napoli in 2013

"Just take a knife and kill me!"

On Liverpool's defence

Klopp on... Liverpool

"We all started playing football against our best friends when we were young and I can't remember a moment when, because it was my best friend, I did not want to win against him. That is absolutely bullsh*t."

On catching up with old friends before Liverpool's match with Dortmund

"If we sit here in four years, I think we win one title. If I don't win the next one, maybe it will have to be in Switzerland."

Klopp pledges to win the Premier League by 2019

"Calm down, it's Christmas?"

Klopp appeals to Sam Allardyce after tensions rise between the Liverpool and Sunderland benches following Jermaine Lens' strong tackle on Reds defender Mamadou Sakho

"It's absolutely not a problem. A lot of people have said worse about me."

Klopp was later called a 'soft German' by Allardyce. The Sunderland manager was surprised Klopp felt the Lens challenge warranted a red card

"I prepare my team, that's why I am here at a place where I had a wonderful time. It is better to be here than, I don't know, North Korea or something. It feels good."

On being the centre of attention returning to his old side Dortmund as Liverpool manager

"I am not a genius. I don't know more than the rest of the world."

The boss has no magic wand when it comes to finding new talent

"I understand derbies. I love derbies. To be honest, it's the salt in the soup."

On the big clash between Liverpool and Man United, also known as North-West derby

"I will not take some pills to stop me from celebrating a goal."

When asked if he'd celebrate the Reds scoring against Dortmund

"There is no solution. We do not have the tallest team in the league. How do you fix that? Make them taller!"

On conceding goals from set-pieces

"Please? Are you crazy? I hope I don't understand the question. I've been here three weeks. You think after one game winning at Chelsea we can win the league?"

Klopp is astounded to be asked about Liverpool's title chances after claiming his first win as manager – a 3-1 success at Chelsea

"Hopefully we'll play better than my understanding of Scouse! It is still pretty difficult for me, especially if somebody speaks as quickly as possible – then I'm completely out!"

On getting to grips with the local dialect

"I usually have a second pair of glasses but I can't find them because it's hard to find glasses without glasses!"

Klopp lost his specs following a crazy touchline celebration when Adam Lallana settled a nine-goal thriller in stoppage time against Norwich

"I look a little bit like a serial killer, but you [the reporter] have ones like that too so you are used to it."

When asked by a reporter if he was sporting new glasses after losing his old pair days earlier at Norwich

"The whole game was not easy. On Thursday we played on ice in Switzerland and today we played a wall with only long balls, with only set plays."

Klopp bemoans West Bromwich Albion's style of football after a 2-2 draw

"Until now it's been OK. I'd really like to change my personality, but I can't forget this f*cking loss against Crystal Palace. If we had won this maybe then I would have said it was more than OK."

Klopp is content with the start to his Liverpool tenure – except for a loss to Crystal Palace

"Because we weren't good enough, the linesman thought, 'You don't make world-class goals if you play this sh*t' so [you don't get the goal]."

Klopp jokes the assistant referee didn't think his side deserved to score after he wrongly flagged Alberto Moreno offside against Newcastle United

"I'm not a dreamer but I'm a football romantic and I love all the stories about this – Anfield is one of the best places for this. Now I'm here, I'm a really lucky guy."

He loves a bit of football romance

"It was not a problem for 10 seconds. We talked about it but I'm not an idiot. For me it's enough that I have the first and last word [on transfers]. I need the other people [on the committee] to get the perfect information."

Klopp insists he is in control of the signings at Liverpool – and not the club's maligned transfer committee

"The dressing room here is not too big, this room is bigger, maybe we should change."

Klopp laments the size of the Exeter dressing room while giving his pre-match media interview – in a tea room

"I am not the guy who is going to go out and shout, 'We are going to conquer the world!' or something like this. But we will conquer the ball, yeah, each f*cking time! We will chase the ball, we will run more, fight more."

The manager outlines his vision at Anfield in typically colourful fashion

"There won't be any problem with the players, as there are also loads of foreign players. My English is probably as bad as theirs so they will understand me a lot easier."

Getting lost in translation at Liverpool is not a worry for Klopp

"We have to talk with all LFC fans. Expectations can be a real big problem. It's like a backpack of 20 kilos. It's not so cool to run with this."

On living up to the hopes of the Liverpool supporters

"I recently met a famous brain surgeon in New York and in his brain, when it comes to intelligence, there are definitely 80 per cent more light bulbs alight than in mine. But what happens? He started to stutter because he is crazy about football and this person from LFC was suddenly standing in front of him."

Klopp on being an idol

"These young players are our future. If we handle them like horses then we get horses."
Referring to Jordan Rossiter who got a hamstring injury while on England U18s duty having played three games in just five days

"If someone is silly enough to want to see my face for 90 minutes during a game, I cannot change the world."
Asked what he thought of 'Klopp Cam' which a German TV station set up to monitor the manager during the 90 minutes of the Reds' match against Dortmund

"I could play them all together. We could play 4-1-4! Hang on, I've forgotten a player haven't I? OK, 4-1-5!"

The boss briefly struggles with his maths when talking tactics against Crystal Palace

"The most difficult thing for me? The two benches being so close. It's so different to Germany. You could accidentally hit the other coach or manager. I get a little bit emotional during a game!"

Klopp is worried about getting a little too personal with the other dugout

"It's OK. They flew, they didn't walk. We slept on the plane. Matt [head of press] slept the whole way!"

On how the long trip to Rubin Kazan in Russia would affect his side

"You have to get information in each situation. You'll never find me three days after a win, drunk in a hedge and still celebrating."

Klopp was asked how Liverpool would recover from defeat to West Ham United and the manager put the result into context

Klopp on... Liverpool

"We had a good plan in the first half but conceded two goals, so you can throw your plan in the purple bin."

The Liverpool boss is unhappy with the goals Dortmund scored against his English side. Purple bin?

"The best word I can say to describe this is: Boom!"

Klopp perfectly sums up the 3-0 triumph over Manchester City

"All I will say is it will be completely different, or not. I won't talk about tactics here. Even in Manchester they have televisions!"

Klopp remains guarded when asked about his plans for the League Cup final against Manchester City

"Until now when I've met an Evertonian, nobody has knocked me, nobody kicked me. It's always nice. Nothing happened."

The boss says he's not experienced any animosity from Everton supporters

Klopp on... Liverpool

"That was the summer?! How can you turn such a positive thing to... oh my God. Really? Yesterday was summer? That means it's autumn again. Urgh."

On being asked if he enjoyed the summer months

"History is only the base for us. It's not allowed that you take the history in your backpack."

Klopp says it's important Liverpool focus on the future and not dwell on past glories

"I'm so happy (jokes). I don't even understand the numbers, what do they mean?"

On Liverpool being 5/1 second favourites for the title

"Please don't ask me about this sh*t because it's so hard."

Klopp responds to being asked if the Reds are a "huge step closer to a trophy" following victory over his old club Dortmund

"It's a year, I'm a year older and all this sh*t, but everything else is good. Not perfect, but in a good way. My year is what, the 8th of October, yes? We will not celebrate, I can tell you that! Hopefully nobody brings me a cake!"

Klopp says he won't be marking his one-year Anfield anniversary

"They did not show this game on TV? They show every f*cking game in Germany."

Klopp complains about the lack of TV coverage of Liverpool's victory against Derby County

"There's no Harry Potter flying on his f*cking stick."

Photo: Michael Hulf

Klopp on... others

"Cristiano [Ronaldo] reminds me of German tennis player Michael Stich. He was destined to make history, but then Boris Becker showed up. Cristiano is so fast, so strong, so incredible, but he has one problem: Leo Messi."

Klopp on the Ronaldo v Messi debate

"He likes having the ball, playing football, passes. It's like an orchestra. But it's a silent song. I like heavy metal."

On the difference between himself and Arsenal manager Arsene Wenger

"All the people told me about the British press, so it's up to you to show me you are all liars."

On the British media's sometimes casual relationship with the truth

"What was the question? Does he like the way I look? I don't think I have a chapter in his book. One chapter: 'How is Klopp looking?'."

On being hip – versus Sir Alex Ferguson being old school

"[Jose] Mourinho says I talk a lot? That's what one of my teachers used to say. I'll shut up, then."

The Normal One on the Special One

"Stop making photos. I go to this side of my room, photograph. I go to the other, photograph. It would be really nice if you leave me there."

Klopp blasts photographers gathered outside his hotel

"They would never wear this club's shirt again. He won't get a second chance to make a mistake like that: 'Look, you might be able to play, but I don't want to see your face again'."

Responding when being asked about Man City's Mario Balotelli, who allegedly threw a dart at a youth team player

"He told me I should leave his player alone and then he said something else which I couldn't hear, which is why I moved in closer. I wasn't looking for new friends. We wanted to win the game and so too did Bayern."

Following a touchline altercation with Bayern director of sport Matthias Sammer

"Bastian Schweinsteiger, shall we say, he hasn't grasped his job perfectly yet."

Klopp pokes fun at the Bayern midfielder's performance after a 1-1 draw

"It was during the most sh*tty moment of my life. I saw him after the Champions League final for two minutes. I met him and he said, 'Great season'. He is unbelievable, unbelievable."

An inspired Klopp on meeting Sir Alex Ferguson after losing the Champions League final to Bayern

"[Lionel] Messi is the best. There must be life out there somewhere, on some other planet. Because he is too good and we are just too bad for him."

On the Barcelona superstar

Bayern president Uli Hoeness: "If I was wearing black-yellow pants, I wouldn't sleep soundly."

Klopp: "Hmm. I wonder what his pants looked like before he went to bed."

"I've never seen you here before. It must be your first time. Which section do you write for again? Nature documentaries?"

Klopp puts down a young reporter

"I'm sure I can have two days and two nights with Sir Alex Ferguson. I don't know what he drinks. Red wine, OK. He can have his red wine. I prefer beer."

On being in Alex Ferguson's company

"Mario woke up this morning with a hardening – in his thigh!"

Klopp is keen to avoid any confusion over the condition of playmaker Mario Gotze

"She wrote a book for children. It's like Harry Potter – but it's about football. There's no Harry Potter flying on his f*cking stick – just football."

On the work of his wife Ulla

"If I were him, I'd thank God that someone had the idea of hiring me every time I walk into the Bayern training ground. I don't know if Bayern would have got one less point without Sammer."

Klopp has a pop at Bayern Munich's sporting director Matthias Sammer

"Crazy players love me – I don't know why."

Klopp on... himself

"I understand television without subtitles, so that is a good thing."

Klopp on moving to England

"Yes, it's true. I underwent a hair transplant. I think the results are really cool, don't you?"

He got a new head of locks in 2012

"I never succeeded in bringing to the field what was going on in my brain. I had the talent for the fifth division, and the mind for the Bundesliga. The result was a career in the second division."

Klopp is philosophical about his abilities as a player

"We still rely on calling the players, and when we make an offer to their agents, they always think that we're making fun of them."

Klopp found it difficult to attract players in Mainz with such a small budget

"I couldn't have been a rock star, although I do sing Country Road very loudly on the PlayStation karaoke game."

Klopp enjoys having a sing-song

"I love to be something like the friend of the player, but not their best friend."

On handling his squad

"My boys sleep in double rooms the night before the match. I hope that nothing happens…"

On whether he bans sex before games

"When I gave the first interview, I was very disappointed. After the second one 10 minutes later, I was feeling better. In 30 minutes, I'll probably feel like we won the match."

Klopp explains how he copes with a defeat

"If you lose a game, everyone asks why this player didn't play. If we win, nobody asks."

The boss is no stranger to football's fickle nature

Klopp on... himself

"I'm a bit proud of my first red card as a coach. I approached the fourth official and said, 'How many mistakes are allowed here? If it's 15, you have one more."

On being sent to the stands

"It doesn't make it any easier to run your heart out when you've just woken up in a five-star hotel. Too much comfort makes you comfortable."

Klopp speaks about the modern footballer

"Usually, I am a really nice guy. But if something pushes the red button, it can happen. And the next problem is my face."

Klopp on his facial expressions

"I am not tired. I may look tired but I am not. I am 0.0 per cent tired."

Klopp after announcing his departure from Dortmund

"My colleagues and I are no magicians. We cannot make good players out of bad players."

On recruiting and developing talent

Klopp on... himself

"No, I make this f*cking face when I play tennis.
That's the truth."

**After getting sent to the stands during a
Dortmund tie against Napoli, the boss says
even away from the pitch, it's quite normal
for him to have an angry face**

"I don't have a problem approaching people,
being nice to the ones who treat me nice. But I
can also be pretty unpleasant when I realise that
a player is not giving me his best in training."

**Klopp expects full commitment from his
players**

"I like the total intensification, when there are crashes and bangs everywhere, a sense of 'all or nothing', pure adrenaline and no one being able to breathe."

On his playing philosophy

"It's not about the money for me. I have enough to eat three times a day!"

Klopp on whether a bumper contract could persuade him to join Chelsea

"I don't remember the plot, but it got right down to business."

He recalls the first time he saw a blue movie

"Usually, I watch everything. The slow horse riding, anything. I have no idea what they are doing, but I like it. I like each kind of sport, every kind of challenge."

Klopp loves watching the Olympics

"It was a joke. I'm not into heavy metal. I mean, I used to like Kiss when I was young, but…"

Klopp sets the record straight about his music taste

"Crazy players love me – I don't know why."

Klopp on being told that he'd get on well with Zlatan Ibrahimovic

"You don't understand? You should learn. There are some really good German explanations for some problems. But I don't know how to say it in English."

The manager tries to get his message across to the British media

"In extreme situations, you have to think fast. At one of my mate's stag parties, we all dressed up as Father Christmas – fully masked."

Klopp tells how he remains discreet when out in public

"With all these pictures on Twitter, it always looks like I am in restaurants and bars. I am not that type of guy."

On attention from social media

"I don't really know how often I shave. There's no regular rhythm. I can't see myself in the mirror in the morning anyway – I'm too short-sighted."

Klopp reveals his shaving habits

"The problem with my life is that I've said too much sh*t in the past and no one forgets it."

The German hilariously admits that past quotes may come back to haunt him

"You drink tea at four o'clock in the afternoon and nobody else knows why in the rest of the world. You drive on the wrong side of the road. We are different."

On life in England

"I've had to put up with poor football for long enough – mainly my own."

Klopp is the master of self-deprecation

Klopp on... himself

"Money isn't the most important thing. It is important, of course. I am not Mahatma Gandhi."

On the importance of money

"Sometimes I frighten myself when I see my touchline antics on TV."

Klopp is all too aware of his eccentric behaviour during games

"My car knows only one way – home to here, here to home. There are more exciting lives around."

The hum-drum nature of his daily routine is not lost on Klopp

"Look, you work for the Guardian, and sometimes you see your colleagues and think, 'Oh no, the same old thing every day.' Maybe you want to go to The Sun? More money, less work. More photographs, fewer words."

When asked by a Guardian journalist about star player Mario Gotze quitting Dortmund for Bayern Munich

"Our pants won't be full. I specifically checked again."

Speaking ahead of a huge Mainz game against Bayern

"I'd have maybe presented some kind of afternoon programme where people aren't all that interested in what you're saying, and you just stare ahead."

Klopp could have been a talk show host had things not worked out in football

"In Germany I look like everyone else. I'm not the best shaver in the world, funny hairstyle, glasses."

On being Jurgen Klopp

"I see you here for the first time and instantly you make demands as to what I should say.... hats off. What department do you work in? Animal movies? Oh sport, oh OK."

When asked by a reporter to not use empty phrases in his answers

"My abilities were somewhat limited in comparison with his…"

Klopp measures his time as a player against that of former Germany striker Jurgen Klinsmann

"Honestly, for me, football is deadly serious for 90 minutes and that's it. The whole circus that's built up around it, the protagonists who are made out to be this, that, or the other – it's all crazy, obviously, and happily I'm smart enough to be able see that for what it is. So I tend to prefer a more humorous approach to the subject."

On being so emotional on the touchline and a joker in the press room

"I don't really want to keep talking about myself."

On the hype of being... Klopp

"If I were working as a bank manager, I might have had a credibility problem, looking like I do, but I don't work as a bank manager. I work in football."

Klopp on his fashion sense

"I like the speed in the game. You have to be a real man or woman in the game. It's hard."

The boss likes the game played at full throttle

"There were 1,500 people there when I left and 1,499 live there now."

Klopp on his hometown of Bretten in the Black Forest

"In England you have stadiums in the middle of the city. We don't have that in Germany. If we had a stadium in the city, the people would be telling you, 'Hey, it's Monday night – turn the sound down'."

Klopp on English football

"The next time, when I've just browbeaten a reporter, then I might be able to tolerate the next three stupid questions and think, 'Come on, you messed up just last week'. But with the fourth stupid question I know without a doubt I'll be on fire again, code red, and the boiler starts overheating."

Klopp admits on he can find it hard to keep his emotions in check with the press

"A doctor, originally. I think I still might have 'helper syndrome' to a certain extent. But I'm not going to lie, I don't think I was ever smart enough for a medical career. When they were handing out our A-Level certificates, my headmaster said to me, 'I hope it works out with football, otherwise it's not looking too good for you'."

On what he wanted to be as a youngster

Q: "Can you tell us what style of play we can expect?"

A: "A wild one"

Klopp on... himself

"Of course! I was a regular customer at the meat counter during the World Cup. I always picked up something for the barbecue."

Klopp was asked if he still goes shopping

"Football is not so important. We don't save lives or things like that. We are not doctors."

He puts the game into perspective

"You'd be waiting 30 or 40 years for me to build a table. I have more than two left hands."

The boss admits he is challenged in the DIY department

"To enjoy football, you have to do this: 'He can win!' 'Then he can win!' 'Post!' 'Goalkeeper!' 'Save!' That is what I love."

Klopp is an emotional guy when it comes to the beautiful game

"Don't say I'm Jesus, then criticise me for not being able to walk on water."

The manager on expectations

"We don't hit each other – but we hit all the other guys."

Klopp on managing people

Klopp on... himself

"My teams don't play football. It's like a game of chess."

His perspective on how football should be played

"Your body makes unbelievable moves. I tore a muscle once celebrating too much."

Talking about his celebrations

"Watch me during the game. I celebrate when we press the ball. Win a throw-in and I say, 'Yessss!'"

Klopp gets fully involved in the action

"You can fall down and then you must stand up. Only silly idiots stay on the floor. We will strike back – 100 per cent."

Fighting talk after Liverpool's defeat to Manchester City in the League Cup final

"If a player doesn't understand the professional part of his life, it is a little bit waste of time."

Klopp won't waste time on players that don't meet his standards

"When I was a kid, when I played tennis, that's how I was. I don't like it, but I have to accept it. If I see a little baby I make the same face. 'Oh come here, how cute you are'."

Explaining why he is so passionate on the touchline

"My mother's probably sitting in front of the television right now, watching this press conference, and not understanding a word I'm saying. But I'm sure she's very proud."

Klopp after being unveiled as new Liverpool manager

"There was real danger I would have to do manual work because there is not so much in here [points to his head]. So I had a good situation that I played at Mainz that they thought maybe it's better he stops and becomes coach of this team."

On how he became a manager

"Great country, great people, good food – just too many matches!"

Describing his first few months in England

Klopp on... himself

"I was very average. I was really quick and [had] a good header but that was it. Unfortunately, the ball spent most of the time on the ground and that was not my biggest strength."

Klopp certainly does not hold his playing abilities in high esteem

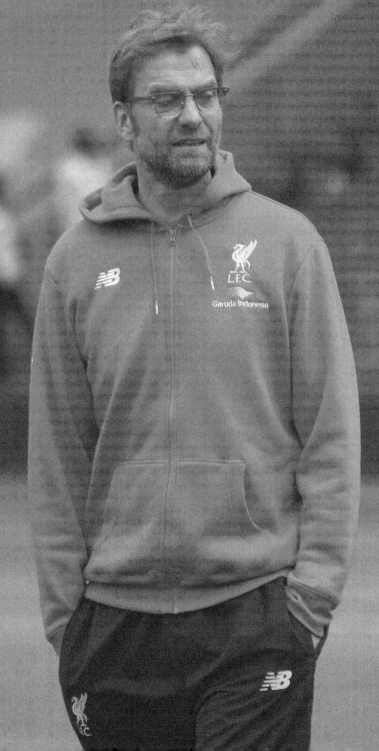

Others...
on Klopp

"He brought tears to everyone's eyes and had mothers holding up their babies, yelling that they would name them after him."

Jan Doehling, a Mainz TV channel producer

"He wants to feel like a 'single manager' and experience things with his wife that he hasn't had time for in a while."

Klopp's agent Marc Kosicke explains why he decided to take a break from football after leaving Dortmund in 2015

"As we say in Germany, you could steal apples and horses with him."

Ex-Dortmund defender Patrick Owomoyela

"He's a soft German if that's a red card. It's a yellow, a foul."

Sam Allardyce responds to Klopp who felt a Jermaine Lens tackle on Mamadou Sakho deserved a straight red

"Is he a bit crazy? Absolutely! He is mad. He can be in so many different moods."

Former Mainz defender Tim Hoogland

"Klopp demonstrated to me perfectly how pressing works using egg cups. That impressed me."

Andreas Rettig, CEO of the German football league

"If Jurgen ever has the good fortune to manage a team like Bayern Munich or Real Madrid, he'll realise what it means, that it's a completely different world."

Bayern boss Jupp Heynckes patronises Klopp after he took a swipe at the way their rivals conduct themselves

"If you see him on the touchlines, that's not emotional. To some extent that has psychopathic excesses."

Ex-Bayern sporting director Christian Nerlinger

"Even if this Mr Klopp always comes out and says, 'Oh sorry'... there's always still something hanging in the air. The kind of behaviour that we have seen from him on many occasions shows such a capacity for aggression that we could see violent excesses at the grassroots level taking their cue from it."

Lutz-Michael Frohlich, head of refereeing at the German FA, is not happy with Klopp

"I believe Klopp is very attractive to women."

Leading brand expert Frank Dopheide

Klopp fact file

I AM THE NORMAL ONE

Full name: Jurgen Norbert Klopp.

Nickname: Kloppo.

Nationality: German.

1967: Born in Stuttgart, on June 16th. He grew up in the Black Forest, in a village close to Freudenstadt.

1987: Began his senior playing career at FC Pforzheim, before moving on to feature for Eintracht Frankfurt's Under-23 side.

1988: He remained in Frankfurt to play for Viktoria Sindlingen the following year.

1989: Klopp was on the move again with a switch to city rivals Rot-Weiss Frankfurt.

Klopp fact file

1990: He became a senior pro after his transfer to Mainz 05. Starting out as a striker before dropping back into defence, he played his entire career here and scored 52 league goals from 337 appearances.

2001: After hanging up his boots at the age of 33, Klopp was installed as Mainz's caretaker coach in February and steered the club away from relegation to the third division. He then became manager and narrowly missed out on promotion to the top flight in 2002 and again in 2003.

2004: The manager finally guided Mainz to the Bundesliga after finishing third in the automatic promotion spots.

2005: Klopp consolidated Mainz's position in Germany's elite division with an 11th-place finish.

2006: It was 11th again for Mainz but Klopp led his side out in the 2005/06 UEFA Cup via the UEFA Fair Play ranking – but they suffered a first-round defeat by eventual winners Sevilla.

2007: At the end of the 2006/07 campaign, Mainz ended up in 16th and were relegated from the Bundesliga.

2008: Klopp stayed loyal but was unable to get Mainz back up and resigned. His record was 109 wins, 78 draws and 83 losses. Named new manager of Borussia Dortmund in May.

Klopp fact file

2009: Guided his new side to sixth place – just missing out on Europe.

2010: The foundations for Dortmund's future success were taking shape after a fifth-place finish and Europa League qualification.

2011: Led Dortmund to the Bundesliga title in 2010/11 for the first time since 2002. Schalke defeated them on penalties in the German Super Cup – the curtain raiser for the following season. Klopp was crowned German Football Manager of the Year.

2012: Klopp won back-to-back titles, with the highest-ever points tally (81). He also made history by claiming the club's first-ever domestic

double after defeating Bayern to win the 2012
German Cup. Klopp won the German Football
Manager of the Year award for the second
successive season.

2013: Dortmund finished runners-up in the
Bundesliga behind Bayern. And their arch
rivals stole a last-gasp victory in the Champions
League final at Wembley. A small consolation
was overcoming Bayern in the German Super
Cup.

2014: Again Dortmund finished second in the
Bundesliga and made it to another German Cup
final – but lost to Bayern. However, Klopp did
secure more silverware with the German Super
Cup by beating their old foes.

Klopp fact file

2015: Klopp left Dortmund at the end of the 2014/15 season to take a sabbatical with the team ending the campaign in seventh. His swansong was a 2015 German Cup final loss to VfL Wolfsburg. Klopp finished his stint as manager with a record of 179 wins, 69 draws, and 70 losses. He cut short his break from football to become the new boss of Liverpool on October 8th, 2015 after replacing Brendan Rodgers.

2016: He guided Liverpool to the 2016 League Cup final but lost out to Manchester City in a penalty shoot-out. In a memorable first season at the helm, Klopp also took the Reds to the Europa League final before losing out to Sevilla 3-1.

Playing career

Youth team

1972–1983   SV Glatten

1983–1987   TuS Ergenzingen

Senior team

1987   1. FC Pforzheim

1987–1988   Eintracht Frankfurt II

1988–1989   Viktoria Sindlingen

1989–1990   Rot-Weiss Frankfurt

1990–2001   Mainz 05

Managerial career

2001–2008   Mainz 05

2008–2015   Borussia Dortmund

2015–   Liverpool

Managerial honours

Borussia Dortmund

Bundesliga: 2010/11, 2011/12.

German Cup: 2011/12.

German Super Cup: 2013, 2014.

Highlights

UEFA Champions League runners-up:

2012/13.

Bundesliga runners-up: 2012/13, 2013/14.

German Cup runners-up: 2013/14, 2014/15.

Led Mainz to the Bundesliga for the first time in

their history in 2004.

FIFA Manager of the Year runner-up: 2013.

German Football Manager of the Year: 2011,

2012.

10 facts on Klopp

1. Klopp has a diploma from the Goethe University of Frankfurt in the field of sports science. His thesis was on race-walking.

2. German comedian Matze Knop paid tribute to Klopp with the songs 'I Wanna Be Like Jurgen Klopp' and 'Kloppo You Rockstar'.

3. Klopp's middle name 'Norbert' means 'shining from the north' or 'shines like the seas'.

4. He's spoken publicly about his Protestant faith.

5. His wife Ulla is a children's book author and was known as the 'First Lady of Bundesliga'.

Klopp fact file

6. Klopp is well regarded for his crazy touchline celebrations and admits he once tore a muscle after one of his players scored.

7. His son Marc played for Borussia Dortmund's U23 youth team before injury ended his career.

8. He is the longest-serving manager at both Mainz (2001-08) and Borussia Dortmund (2008-15) and has never been sacked.

9. The manager's flowing locks are from a hair transplant he had in 2012.

10. Klopp often walked home from Dortmund's stadium after matches. He said it gave him time to ponder how his side had played.

I AM THE NORMAL ONE

8275443R00077

Printed in Germany
by Amazon Distribution
GmbH, Leipzig